OF MONSTERS
AND MADNESS

CHARLIE EDGAR

Drunken Pirate Publishing

OF MONSTERS AND MADNESS

Dedication

For those who feel the need to hide their pain.

Drunken Pirate Publishing
ISBN: 979-8-218-03865-6
First Printing, 2022

Is This Where I Put The Trigger Warning?

This is not a happy book, or so i've been told. These musings do not end with happily ever after. There is no prince/princess hiding away in a tall castle, nor is there someone waiting to rescue them. For that is the stuff of fairytales. This collection resides far from happily ever after because life itself is not that kind. The various prose contained within these pages can be dark and triggering for some; others may read them and wonder why a trigger warning was included at all. I decided to include one out of respect for the journey. I don't know what you've been through so all I can do, one human to another, is let you know that some of what you are about to read was born within a dark place. A place where the sting of anger and betrayal lay fresh and the only resolution for my survival was to put pen to paper and let the ink bleed it out.

tell me a story of monsters and madness
for i've grown tired of their lies...

It's rare in modern existence to find a person wholly untouched by greed, deceit, or violence. At birth life is full of possibility and promise, but soon experience chips away at our innocence as we struggle to carry the weight of generational trauma.

If left to its own devices pain will cause one to languish in denial, anger, fear, and self-loathing as it slowly decimates the psyche to the point where our actions are not entirely our own for they are built upon a foundation of learned response.

Trauma cares not for class, ethnicity, nor education and those who think they can escape it are either naïve or lying for the evolution of society itself is rife with stories of empires built upon the backs of others and sustained by little more than force-fed ideals and no other choice. These civilizations, conceived within the womb of power utilized hate and fear to control and manipulate the masses; and not much has changed.

Each day we watch societal divides grow while world leaders hide behind thinly veiled excuses weaving tapestries from the thread of racism and classism.

So, we search for God, yet the road to salvation is paved with the blood and bones of those who dared to question. Using his name, they ignore and ostracize his children. They stand under the cover of neon lights, atop high-rise stages pointing to the opulence paid for from the thinned pocketbooks of the faithful.

Humanity steals in the name of progress and kills under the guise of protection, but an 'eye for an eye' has truly made the whole world blind, and it's here within that darkness of the human experience, where monsters are made. So, we have no other choice than to spin wildly into the madness, looking for something to save us.

the darkness of her silhouette pales in comparison
to the darkness in her eyes
but that's what bitterness does to you
it slowly extinguishes your flame leaving you blind and lost
alone in your misery until nothing remains
but the shallowness of your final breath

time is a thief that
cannot be stopped
and fear a monster that steals from you slowly
and those small moments of indecision
that you thought were only seconds
are now millions of stolen smiles

the most tragic of all
is you have the power to stop it
but you allow fear
to tie you to an existence you despise

so I beg of you
stand up
fight
don't allow another moment to be stolen
don't allow your flame to be extinguished
allow it to illuminate the night.

they tell you she is unkind
that her words are lies
propelled by a rage within the misery of her soul
yet she watched for decades
as their twisted, misguided words
manipulated everything she holds sacred

call it what you will but when your
livelihood is earned through
the generosity of a parish
your purpose is muddied

for by His stripes
His story pays your bills

clothed in luxury as your people starve
you twist your words and use regurgitated ideology
to indoctrinate those who will not question
molding the same three scriptures from the holy text
to justify the end to your means

since His death
man has found ways to market His message for profit
intertwining His words into their political agendas
controlling the masses through fear

this is why He turned over tables of the religious
this is why we should do the same.

in that moment
I saw through you
hiding in the corner of your eye
was the truth
the truth that it wasn't me
it was anyone
so i sat back and listened
as you recycled conversation
articulating your desires as daydreams
just beyond your grasp
and it was in that moment
my fondness for you faded
then you leaned over
and kissed my cheek
a glimpse of vulnerability
before turning away
and my heart ached for something
that never truly existed

I think you broke me
not all of me
that would be absurd
but a small part
tucked away in a corner
with smoke, whiskey, and low light
as music played
and cleverly chosen words dismantled walls
and I found myself in a place I never thought i'd be
I found myself no longer wanting to be alone

there is a sadness in her laughter
for death has whispered in her ear far too many times...

He lay motionless, the pain in his head radiating in tandem with the flicker of the neon sign. His shirt once crisp and new, is now dirty and torn, and even the forcefulness of the recent downpour couldn't rid him of his smell. For most, he's nothing but a prop that's fading into the backdrop of a city with better things to do than pay attention. And why would they notice, for he lay among overfilled trash cans and discarded waste tucked deep within a darkened ally where most dare not go. His current predicament is a sad metaphor of a life poorly lived.

Slipping in and out of consciousness, unnoticed and ignored his resentment grows. "Give me your tired, your poor, your huddled masses..." he sneers. Words that once rang true are now a mockery of the self-indulgent monster it longed to avoid. Truth is, the great Colossus has fallen, and he is a by-product of its destruction as it clings to outdated ideals and industrial age reasonings. Taught to never question, God nor country, he pledged allegiance to the flag and fought for the republic for which it stands. He shed blood, sweat and tears on shores both foreign and domestic, but when the wars stopped and the factories closed, they remained silent. When the battles he faced moved from distant shores of enemy terrain to the darkness of his mind they abandoned him and left him to die; for a life of service, vilification his only reward.

"Where is your country? Where is your god?" He bellows. "Go live in your bubbles and put coins in the collection plates you puppets, as if that alone will save your souls."

I feel strangely about love
a concept romanticized
throughout history
from the unrequited
to the soulmate
never has a topic been so misunderstood

born from biology
and nurtured within fairytales
the archetype is far from the truth
for it lingers in the shallows
ignoring the reality
that happily ever after
is a misnomer
and the depths of love
are far too terrifying
to put into
children's books

it's not a sadness
it's altogether a different feeling
one that cannot be remedied with anything
simplistic or uncomplicated
an amalgam of self-loathing and trauma
this pain belongs to the soul
in the untouchable corners
that are often overlooked
but i've wrestled it within the shadows of neglect
i learned its face
and i called its name
now it waits
angry and caged
acknowledged and
understood

give me melancholy magic
give me liquor that burns
for I want to keep company with the truth
before the music stops and I am told
by those who do not understand my pain
that life is not that serious
and happiness is nothing more than a choice

a skeleton comprised of betrayals
bones created from the stories of
generations who have gone before us
hidden under layers of muscle and skin
good or bad each journey is
embedded into the fabric of our existence

walking through life with
your mothers angst
your fathers rage
your grandparents propensity for alcoholism

these are the things no one mentions
because the truth is ugly
and their struggles
are passed to the next generation

the only way out is through the truth
and even then not every wrongdoing can be fixed
only understood

she stands near the edge of desire
an intensity conceived within
the small moments of each day
it guides every decision that has led her to this place
she bites her bottom lip
to distract from the gravity of the moment
but nothing can calm the flutters in her soul
as she moves closer to the edge
every step deepens her desire
she feels his presence
his breathing labored
as he reaches for her
pulling her into his arms
opening her eyes
she gazes over the mountains edge
as the sea rages against the sharpened rocks below
watching the violent nature that was to
be her end
"I know living is difficult" he whispers
"but please, don't stop"

navigating a roadmap of scars
each sin carved into his skin for all to see
whispers they thought discreet
slowly and methodically
slice their way into his psyche
dismantling his defenses
until the person he once was
is no longer recognizable
and the youthful glow has all but vanished
and there is nothing left
except the hollowness of his eyes

upon on gilded thrones you sit
high above the crowds
a carefully constructed distance
far from the actuality of a world torn in two
giving to those in need but only if its marketable
smile for the camera
don't forget the hashtags
your message is hollow and self-serving
don't go outside the walls
its dirty out there
adherence to your dogma
at the cost of humanity
it's all a fraud

she kneels before the altar
but her answer tarries
there must be a sacrifice
freedom always requires a price
she waits for a lamb to appear
yet she is far removed from
Old Testament scripture

to become the
person she needs
she must kill
the person she was
she must
light the pyre
and watch it burn

Her rape was not a violent one. That is what they said for there was no bruising, at least none visible upon inspection nor was he a stranger lurking in the shadows. He was a friend. One that protected her and kept her safe. Those memories are now gone. The only thing that remains are the nightmares.

Crowds gathered to mark years of freedom for God and country, and while the night sky danced with the glitter and gold of gunpowder shells, her body was paralyzed under the weight of his sin as her objections were masked by the cannon fodder of celebration.

So no, there was no skin under her nails nor bruising on her thighs nevertheless it destroyed her.

we rage against injustices
and war against atrocities
but only within the construct
of character count and trending topics
placing ourselves within their algorithm
humanitarianism packaged within
sixty second increments
as a sound byte of careful selection
gives meaning to our metrics
feeding a machine of their creation
as we search for truth
within carnival house mirrors
but only after a word from
our sponsor

she carries her wars with her
not of blood nor steel
but of experience
of lessons learned
from falling from mountains
she spent a lifetime trying to climb

now standing
on the other side
of youthful naivety
she is steadfast
breathing in
the air of freedom
and it burns her
lungs

i am not afraid
of the madness
i do not fear unending thoughts
nor the nightmares that wreak havoc
on my slumber
i fear wasting time
no, it's not the deathbed
that frightens me
but the weight of indecision
and the yoke of regret
it's the longing to live fully
but failing to do so
that chokes every breath

it's dark inside the box
fashioned with ill intent and clay
misery and pain move as lions starved of freedom
disease and dread create songs of anguish
as the gnashing of teeth builds melodies of suffering

songs meant not for the empty crevices of the nonexistent
but for the unknowing souls waiting just outside
a gift designed by the gods

      oh Pandora do you not know
      one should never accept a gift from the gods

yet the fickle nature of humanity is insatiable
so the lid is removed

suffering has many names but none as
wearisome as the one left behind

      oh, the troublesome toil of hope
      with its endless wonder and selfish gains
      too heavy a burden to unleash upon
      humanity for they are not strong enough to carry it

Decades have passed since my feet crossed the threshold of the rustic, A-frame structure. Once a brightly colored symbol of hope is now faded and showing signs of age. A simplistic beauty and quintessentially humble its walls house a multitude of memories, A place where rambunctious children carved trails of boredom into wooden pews with ink-less pens. Each grove holding the remnants of disapproving glances from old ladies in large hats. The type of hats only worn in the South where sweet tea flows freely and each Sunday service ends with a buffet of fried chicken and potato salad.

Thin coats of white paint do little to hide years of abuse on battered baseboards left by the patent leather shoes of the faithful that danced their way down the aisles. Vaulted ceilings held together by wooden beams now house dust and cobwebs as the sunlight casts a myriad of colors reflected through stained-glass windows that depict sinner and saint alike. Flooded with waves of nostalgia my eyes fill with tears for this is a place of innocence, this is the place where I met God.

Standing within the silence I feel a hand reach for mine. She has the same white hair and floral print dress; simple and casual just as I remember. Her presence brings a peacefulness as her spirit breaks through the decades that separate us.

She doesn't say anything, she doesn't have to as the bond between grandmother and grandchild is one that needs no words. And within this moment I am taken back to a time before the chaos of trauma touched my skin. I want to savor every minute. I want to stop time from moving. I want to tell her that despite everything, I don't blame her. I want to let her know that I'm okay, and that life has taught me to be strong.

She turns to me and smiles, an acknowledgement of knowing wrapped in a million unspoken words lost to time and circumstance. And as quickly as she appeared, she was gone and I was alone with the responsibility of time.

Turning to leave I stop to take one last look, when I see her; with a sunlight halo and blonde ringlets stands the small child I once was, and she was smiling and I knew that despite everything she would face

she would be okay.

i don't hate you
i've put you in a much darker place
a place within my soul where emotion does not exist
no joy
nor sorrow
no pleasure
nor pain
you lay within a faceless sarcophagus
wrapped in the sins of your existence
as you fade into the nothingness of forgotten memory

we tip-toe through conversational land mines
swallowing time bombs of anger wrapped obligation
as gunpowder kegs of resentment
teeter on the edge of matchstick ledges
I watch you hold fast to the illusion that ignorance is bliss
and I find myself wishing
that our brokenness was the same
because I envy you
I want the ability to bury emotion and memory
because trauma doesn't matter
when its wrapped in smiling Polaroids
of Christmas trees and old toys
keep up the illusions
it's easier than the truth.

i asked for compassion and my heart broke as
the of veil of self was lifted
I watched as one by one
with eyes sewn shut
they walked blindly into the abyss
screaming for salvation
but there is no solace
for the imprisoned
as hate and despair
guard its gates
hell is a manner of existing
and for those who journey through it
peace is nothing more than the construct
of late-night infomercials and brown liquor
compassion is not for the weak
for with it comes anger at those who remain silent
indifference and fear build more walls
than our government ever will
and to channel this anger
requires the composure of someone
i fear I can never be

there are miracles inside of you
a universe of untapped potential
it will not be easy
you must fight every instinct to run
and every desire to recoil from life
you will be scared
you will be hurt
but one day it will all
make sense
and your pain
will serve a purpose
and once it does
you will never look back

welcomed as a friend
each one pacifies a part of me broken long ago
freedom waits in the most mundane of places
next to the coffee pot and breadcrumbs
20 mg of happiness
40 mg of pay attention
10 mg of calm the fuck down
each day working to rewire the physiology of my existence
hope is the opiate of the masses
produced and distributed
to those who are willing
to pay the piper
robbing Peter to pay Paul
but does it matter where
the money comes from
if this pill can save your soul

the normalcy of Big Pharma
numb the symptoms
and place the solutions out of reach
once swearing by Apollo the Physician
their oath faded from memory long
ago as they are too far
removed from the face of their
decisions
for they profit from our
sickness playing
puppeteer with our lives

the familiar can be a cruel place
tying you to an existence
where you no longer belong

we all give up something
with each decision
we choose our adventure
building for ourselves the lives we are living
yet despite what is gained
long after the initial flutters of newness have passed
there is a crushing reality that soon hits
and we find ourselves in that space
where the realization
that dopamine fueled decisions
have warped our perspectives
and what we once desired
has become tiresome
and mundane
and the familiarity that once comforted
is now the seed that breeds contempt
and sometimes there are no answers

my heart is heavy
the weight of trauma leaving a void that
empties me of everything that is good
i wander through abandoned woods searching

yet i grow weary

I sit next to concrete headstones
whose monikers are no longer visible
and it is there in the stillness
where I find rest

you're a mess dear child
  chaos overflowing from a cup

trying to fit into the delicate porcelain
    with the peonies and golden lip

you spill from its sides like ocean waves
    against hardened rocks

but that is where you belong
  outside of the delicate
      outside of the pristine
          for in your wildness is your truth

the betrayals seem so small
but that's how deeply I trusted you
i showed you every scar
as we dissected every wound
yet you remained silent when they cursed my name
there is nothing just in this Holy war

i do not want to think of time nor age
for these topics are far too fleeting
i want to know what awakens your soul
i want to know what you think of
as you wander the earth
for we are not bound by
the social
constructs of time
so let us drink in
the wonder of
conversation
and bask in all
that life has to
offer

restlessness sets in
always longing for what is next
as a million failures lay scattered
in the wake of my existence
a place where city streets
are paved with the bones of discarded dreams
routine and consistency are a noose around the neck
standing atop a platform of responsibility
there's a small pause
before the platform drops
lay my body with the rest of them
may it help pave the roads
that lead out of this place

there is a moment where death
becomes more than a concept
when it reaches
from beyond the eventual
into the inevitable
and the recollection of a life well lived
scatters across broken memory
as the shadow of an existence
once pressed firmly into your story
begins to fade
and to remember
how it felt
to sit beside them
is lost to the abyss of time

sauntering through halls of acceptance
i am a curator of my suffering
each moment carefully encased within
the ornate framework of my choosing
a private museum no one cares to go
yet they peek through windows
and cracked doors
whispering with sideways glances
not knowing that their voices amplify beyond the
social construct of their fake smiles
and false encouragement
so strange and content in her misery
but my truth lay far from
preconceived notions of melancholy
i do not savor suffering
i take pride in survival
i point to the brokenness
not to revel in the shattered pieces
but to show that existence
beyond pain is possible

alone in a vast universe of his own creation
a prisoner
locked within
the deafening silence
of space and time
waiting for their
moment of inevitability
it's an experience so destructively beautiful
it defines everything he touches
every road he travels
every word he speaks
all fueled by the remnants of her existence
yet every story has its end
and what was once
the light that guided him
is now a whisper of a memory
fading into the unavoidable pathos
that is nostalgia

we hunger for truth
demand knowledge
not expecting the bitter taste of the fruit we have chosen
for the truth was found buried under blood soaked soil
watered by genocidal rage
it was plucked from under the trees
of white washed history
as the sky rained with the ash of the witches that burned
proselytizing atop stolen lands
while sacred sites were desecrated for profit
as children whose homes were stolen
were forced to recite "with liberty and justice for all"
because cruelty is okay if it's ordained by God
so let us burn the history books
let them be rewritten with the truth
for while we cannot change the past
it's time we faced it

not long ago
we ran through wooded forests
building forts inside abandoned cars
that had rusted-out bottoms
and missing windows
a fortress found within the juxtaposition
of nature and machine
we created stories and chased sunlight
until fireflies illuminated the dark
and then life
with its storm's and terror
stole from us our innocence
replacing it with responsibility and heartache
caught within
the current of time
we ran until there was nothing left
but the memory
of who we once were

my sober heart won't hear you
so let us drink
until liquor washes away memory
as you tell me
all the ways you're sorry
for only in those moments
do I believe you

living between the lines of prose
and swimming within the depths of nuance
is a manner of survival

you are my biggest lie
created with the pages of a book
only read by me
you are not real
you never were
an amalgam of everything
I thought I wanted
but the truth is
you are a fallacy
created to keep me safe
but now the monster created to protect me
is holding me prisoner
chaining me to an existence i never intended

i hold on too tightly
clinging to faded dreams with a grip so intense
any chance of life has slipped away
i don't want to be her
but i can't let her go

because letting her go
means lowering her permanently
into a casket of what once was
and that's a pain
i'm not ready to face

there is a place
in our life
between truth
and action
that is filled with
all the ways
we are told to be

we all have our secrets
stories hidden within our hearts
we carry them with us
some too precious to share
others too dark to reveal
within those stories
are the roadmaps that led us here

it's distasteful becoming a writer
you see it on the faces of everyone who asks
what it is you do for a living
i blame it on the beat generation
with their free love and acid-induced shenanigans
their writing left us a path sullied
with the stench of disappointment and societal disgust

i suppose by now most are dead
or living in a urine-soaked cardboard box
holding fast to their principles and nothing more
those that etched a name for themselves
are the ones bathed in whiskey and sin

while the others lay six feet beneath a cold stone marker
after tasting the ash of a shotgun shell
seems like such a tragic waste
yet those who were born with ink in their veins
they crave it

a sad destructive path
forged in the fires of turmoil
trails laced with
the broken remains
of once held dreams
now bound to the dirt
with typewriter ribbon shackles

it's a sham of an existence

and the only thing separating the successful
from the shotgun brigade
is the thin line of
topical commentary

to write from experience
with its carnage and trauma
re-living it each day
this is where
madness lies
this is where
monsters are made

I stand near your grave
at least that is what I am told
for there is no marker
because a vow was made
that you would not be remembered

death was too easy for you
it was merciful and swift
i wish you would have lived
so you could look me in the eyes as I am now
and answer for your sins
in the end you were spared
for death is far kinder than I

i hate knowing you sleep peacefully
the thought of your indifference
brings a rage that cannot be undone
each day i fight wars
started by the fragility of ego
as forgive and forget is force fed
past clenched jaws and gritting teeth
and I am tired
weary from carrying the weight
of others' mistakes
as half-truths hang in the air
I walk through trails of reason
with gas lit lanterns
holding out hope that
at the end of this journey
it will no longer hurt

lost within the space between faith and fear
there was no solace nor protection
only the omission of truth
as those meant to guide
watched idly as her soul carried
the darkness of those moments
they watched as she walked
through the valley of the shadow of death
alone
battered
bruised
her feet now blistered from
burned bridges she choses to never cross again
it's not that they didn't see her
it's that in their eyes
she was never worth saving

It is no longer yours to carry
like all dead things it belongs elsewhere
six feet underground
or sealed within a tomb
so release yourself from its burden
allow the ground to swallow it
and turn it back to dust
allow the earth to claim it
and bring your life back to a state of order
for in the process of evolution
every season has its end
and if you tie yourself
to that which is dead
the decay will consume you

there is a symmetry to nature
a balance to the cosmos
and from that chaos comes order
so i urge you
sit within the uncomfortable
not to wallow within its shadows
but to learn its origins
to see its face
and within it
you will find the mysteries
that have created you

I will never understand the word lonely
for in my mind I have lived a thousand lifetimes
and I would rather be there
alone
a single star
trapped in a distant galaxy
than surrounded by masses
discussing banal topics with fake laughter

My words lay as wreckage
a chaos of linguistic design
my only hope for survival
is a blank page and time

do not tell me to
"choose happiness"
as if I can wander through an orchard of emotion
plucking happiness from a tree
only to watch as the fruit turns to ash in my hand
for it is not my happiness you are concerned with
I have discovered that "choose happiness"
means be quiet
for you are more disturbed
by the anger within the reaction
than by the abuses that have led to this place
and that screams louder
than I ever could

I don't ascribe to the notion
that life must be routine
wake up
shower
go to work
mow the lawn on the weekends
and try to have a hobby or two
doing the same thing day in and day out for thirty years
until society says you're no longer useful.
It's a slow march towards the grave all because
somewhere along the line we lost our nerve
so we break our bones
and grind our dreams to dust
because someone in a corner office
told us that is the existence we should want
and we don' t dare to question because
we are scared to ask ourselves the hard questions
more-so we are scared of the answers
now if this is what makes you happy
then drink in your champagne wishes
with your caviar chaser
as you count the days between mortgage payments
but don't belittle those
who no longer want to chain themselves
to the misery of the money machine

Fear is a constant companion.
It is the monster that lives under the bed
and within the shadows of each day.
Hidden under layers of subconscious thought,
with its mangled teeth and sharpened claws,
it bore into my soul
whispering from the face of every stranger.
I was not shy.
I was scared.
There were moments of peace
that eased the burden of knowing
knowing that beneath the denial
there was an evil residing within his soul
and all it took was one look in his direction
and the fear I had forgotten
would come flooding back
and I would charge forward
locking every door and closing every curtain
cowering in the closet
hoping with every wish upon a star prayer I could muster
that he couldn't see me hiding within the shadows
behind old books and discarded dolls.
At night, my eyes betrayed my senses
as nightmares were made manifest,
each breath a struggle until the dawn,
but even the light held its own ghosts.
"People who hate others go to hell."
This was my understanding,
so my fate was sealed before my life was lived.

Word of his death arrived.
A gift wrapped in paralyzing hope.
Asked to call upon our faith for the best possible outcome
I ran to my room, fell to my knees, and prayed it was true.

As I grew the memory of those events faded.
Reduced to a bad dream broken into forgotten pieces.
Repression shielding a trauma so convoluted
two broken narratives looped within my mind.
One, a happy childhood filled with smiles and laughter
as we played endlessly in the summer sun
while the warmth of the day sent
beads of sweat down our brow.
The other, a dark story told to an audience of one
Where self-disgust reigned supreme
and the ghost of stories untold
defined what it means to be afraid.

Like all unbreakable things
strength is forged
in the darkest parts of life
tested within the battles of existence
and solidified when you
refuse to allow its rage to consume you

we are made of different things
i am made of broken bones and fragments of worn out skin
stitched together with a thread of rage
my dreams are not like yours
they are
dark
twisted
there is no good in them
for they are a reflection of me
you are everything i am not
so run
fast and far
before these demons drag you to hell with me

a void grows deep within my soul
and with each passing moment
my internal clock is counting down
to my inevitable implosion
tick-tick-tick
a single moment in time when my universe will shatter
for i am hell bent on self destruction
so i wait
as the sound of my failures
reverberate though my mind
drinking cocktails of self loathing
as clouds of regret billow from my lungs

I watched as you tripped
falling into madness
watching as you self destruct at every turn
until I was convinced
you were addicted to the pain
I made no effort to save you
it was easier for me to watch you fall
because in the end you believe that they were right
and that you weren't worth saving
but I'm still here
that small part of you
that is not afraid of the evil
the part of you that is not afraid of the fight
but you have to believe I exist
and when you do
there is nothing they can do to stop you
so please
I beg of you
remember me

there's so much noise it hurts my soul
that's the only way I know to describe it
monetization under the guise of connection
it all feels fraudulent

There will come a day
when the energy will shift
doors will close
and those who once stood at your side
are no longer in view
and that's okay
let summer be put to rest
and let the trees make ready for fall
do not allow yourself to cling to a season
that has long since passed

she dances among the ruins
a million tiny embers lay scattered at her feet
as the smoke billows across the remnants of what they had
built
holding the torch she twirls in the moonlight
laughing at their disbelief
she warned it wasn't just the bridges that would burn
vengeance wasn't for her alone
but for the others
and for those yet to come

Oh how I crave silence
a small slice of heaven
before the world stirs
and the air is filled with
inflection laced banter
and hidden context
I want to bottle those moments of peace
carry them with me
and drink from it
for now disassociation is my shelter
as i have been taught that human nature
cannot be trusted

                                          so i run
                              run far from human connection
                          run far from anything that can hurt
                                        i am only safe
                                         while I run

you can find me
among coffee ring stained book covers
and in the empty spaces of broken book spines
with dog-eared pages
and receipt tape book marks
sitting in dusty bookstores
sifting through stories
that are told by disillusioned old men
after too much whiskey
and not enough sleep
I am searching for something hidden long ago
I am searching for the truth

we are taught that evil resides in the dark,

because that is where they keep their secrets...

About The Author
Charlie Edgar is an author residing within a constant state
of chaotic thought.
I could go on, but in all actuality who reads
'About The Author' pages anyway?

If you or someone you know is struggling, or has concerns about their mental health, there are ways to get help.

National Suicide Prevention Lifeline

Call 988

The Lifeline is a free, confidential crisis service that is available to everyone 24 hours a day, seven days a week. The Lifeline connects people to the nearest crisis center in the Lifeline national network. These centers provide crisis counseling and mental health referrals.

Crisis Text Line

Text "HELLO" to 741741

The Crisis Text hotline is available 24 hours a day, seven days a week throughout the U.S. The Crisis Text Line serves anyone, in any type of crisis, connecting them with a crisis counselor who can provide support and information.

Veterans Crisis Line

Call 1-800-273-TALK (8255) and press 1 or text to 838255

Use Veterans Crisis Chat on the web

The Veterans Crisis Line is a free, confidential resource that connects veterans 24 hours a day, seven days a week with a trained responder. The service is available to all veterans, even if they are not registered with the VA or enrolled in VA healthcare.

Call 911 if you or someone you know is in immediate danger or go to the nearest emergency room.